Do you paint in martial arts?

T0337086

Written by Tom Ottway

Illustrated by Leo Campos

Collins

What's in this book?

Listen and say

Taekwondo

Judo

Karate

Download the audio at www.collins.co.uk/839822

Kung Fu

Tai Chi

🎧 "Zim, come to my martial arts club with me," said Lisa.

Do you paint in martial arts?

4

"No, Zim! That's very funny!" said Lisa.
"You don't *paint*! Martial arts are sports.
You *fight* in different ways."

"Oh!" said Zim.

"Which martial art is the best, Lisa?" asked Zim.

"I don't know. There are many. There's Karate, Taekwondo, Kung Fu, Judo and Tai Chi," said Lisa.

"Karate is great," said Lisa.

"Why?" asked Zim.

"You use your body and you think. You kick with your feet and move your hands like this," said Lisa. "A lot of people do Karate."

"Is Karate your favourite martial art?" asked Zim.

Hmmm ...

"I like Taekwondo too. It's a difficult martial art but a lot of people do it," said Lisa.

"Why is it difficult?" asked Zim.

"You use your hands and your feet in lots of different moves," said Lisa.

"You learn a lot of different ways to kick and it's very fast."

"It looks very fast!" says Zim.

"Would you like to try Judo, Zim?"
asked Lisa. "In Judo, you don't kick, you
hold the other person."

"You don't want them to move."

"Is this Judo, too?" asked Zim.

"No, this is Tai Chi," said Lisa. "Tai Chi is different. Tai Chi is about balance. This boy is balancing on one leg. It's good for your body and helps you think," said Lisa.

"Is it fast?" asked Zim.

"No," said Lisa. "It's very slow."

"I like balancing," said Zim. "This person is balancing, too. Is he doing Tai Chi?"

"No, he's doing Kung Fu," said Lisa. "Kung Fu is very different! Sometimes it's slow and sometimes it's fast.

You balance and move your hands.
Then you move fast and you kick with
your feet or strike with your hands!
It's very exciting," said Lisa.

I like that!

"The people are wearing special clothes. What are they?" asked Zim.

jacket

trousers

"You often wear a white jacket, white trousers and a belt," said Lisa. "You start with a white belt. You finish with a black belt when you are very good!"

I want a black belt!

belt

"Lots of people do martial arts.
"Judo, Taekwondo and Karate are in the
Olympic Games," said Lisa.

19

"So, Zim, which martial art do you like best?" asked Lisa.

"I'm not very fast. I like slow and quiet sports," said Zim.

"I can balance, so I think Tai Chi is the martial art for me!" said Zim.

"That's great," said Lisa.

"But not with paints!" said Zim.

Picture dictionary

Listen and repeat

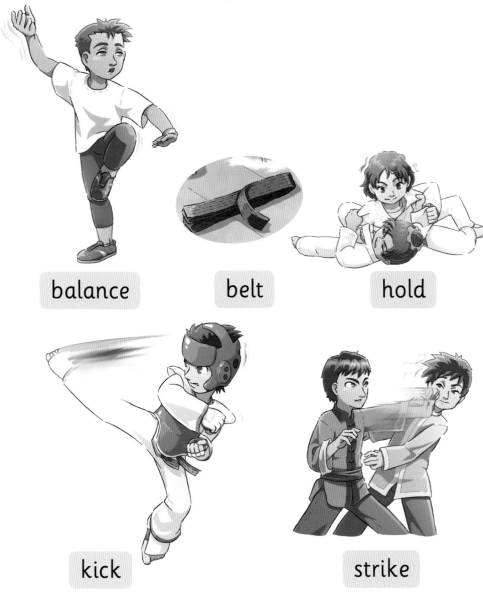

balance   belt   hold

kick   strike

1 Look and match

Kung Fu   Tai Chi

Taekwondo   Judo

2 Listen and say

Collins

Published by Collins
An imprint of HarperCollins*Publishers*
Westerhill Road
Bishopbriggs
Glasgow
G64 2QT

HarperCollins*Publishers*
1st Floor, Watermarque Building
Ringsend Road
Dublin 4
Ireland

William Collins' dream of knowledge for all began with the publication of his first book in 1819.

A self-educated mill worker, he not only enriched millions of lives, but also founded a flourishing publishing house. Today, staying true to this spirit, Collins books are packed with inspiration, innovation and practical expertise. They place you at the centre of a world of possibility and give you exactly what you need to explore it.

© HarperCollins*Publishers* Limited 2020

10 9 8 7 6 5 4 3 2

ISBN 978-0-00-839822-4

Collins® and COBUILD® are registered trademarks of HarperCollins*Publishers* Limited

www.collins.co.uk/elt

British Library Cataloguing in Publication Data

A catalogue record for this publication is available from the British Library.

Author: Tom Ottway
Illustrator: Leo Campos (Beehive)
Series editor: Rebecca Adlard
Publishing manager: Lisa Todd
Product managers: Jennifer Hall and Caroline Green
In-house editor: Alma Puts Keren
Project manager: Emily Hooton
Editor: Barbara MacKay
Proofreaders: Natalie Murray and Michael Lamb
Cover designer: Kevin Robbins
Typesetter: 2Hoots Publishing Services Ltd
Audio produced by id audio, London
Reading guide author: Emma Wilkinson
Production controller: Rachel Weaver
Printed and bound by: GPS Group, Slovenia

MIX
Paper from
responsible sources
FSC™ C007454

Download the audio for this book and a reading guide for parents and teachers at www.collins.co.uk/839822